Travel Journal
Greece

VPJournals

Copyright © 2015 VPJournals

All rights reserved.

ISBN-13: 978-1518845345
ISBN-10: 1518845347

Contact Details

Name:

Email address:

Tel:

Address:

Important Medical Information

Blood type:

Medication:

CONTENTS

Hi, I hope you enjoy this journal. It is packed with cool stuff and recommendations for you trip to Greece, and has plenty of space to record details of your trip.

What's Inside   Page

Before you go to Greece
Great places to visit in Greece   6-7
Cool places to visit in Greece with kids   8-9
Good places to eat   10-11
Research Greece   12-13
Postcard & Packing List   14-19
Greece facts   21-22

Helpful hints   23-26
Clothes and shoe sizing charts, to help you get the right sizes while there

Greece Trip Diary   27-111
21 day trip diary to record details of your trip

Reflect on you Trip
Summary of your trip   113-121
People you met   123-125

Useful Resources   127-136
Size conversion charts   129-132
Common Translations   133-134
Notes   135-136

Have fun in Greece

Great Places to visit in Greece

National Archaeological Museum	✓
Temple of Poseidon	
Navagio Beach (Shipwreck Beach)	
Balos Beach and Lagoon	
Kassiopi	
Open Air Cinema Kamari	
The Acropolis Museum	
Porto Katsiki	
Acropolis of Lindos	
Plaka	
Byzantine Museum (Vizantino Museo)	
Panathenaic Stadium	

Church of Panagia Evangelistria	
Spinalonga (Kalydon)	
Parthenon	
Matoyianni Street	
Medieval City	
Temple of Hephaestus	
Akrotiri Archaeological Site	
Botanical Park Of Crete	
Palace of the Grand Masters	
The Palace of Knossos	
Lychnostatis Museum	
Plateia Miaouli	
Museum of Contemporary Art	

Cool Places to visit in Greece with Kids

Attica Zoological Park	✓
Cretaquarium	
National Marine Park - Alónnissos	
Hellenic Children's Museum	
Allou Fun Park	
Petaloúdes (Butterfly Valley)	
Museum of Greek Children's Art	
National Garden of Athens	
Goulandris Natural History Museum	
Smart Park	
Hellenic Children's Museum	
Cultural Park	

National Marine Park - Zákynthos	
Karavi Schinias	
Acqua Plus Water Park	
The Water Park	
Cretaquarium Thalassocosmos	
Watercity	
Aquaworld Aquarium	
Athens Clue	
Samaria Gorge National Park	
The MindTrap	
Lido Waterpark	
Star Beach Water Park	
Tsilivi Waterpark	

Good Places to Eat in Greece

Leonidas & Panagiota	✓
Paradise Beach	
Levantis	
Sapore Cucine Italiana	
Kolyvata Taverna	
Spondi	
Thea	
Ermis	
Captain Dimos	
Skoufias	
Taverna Piteros	
The Nest	

Klimataria	
Ferryman Taverna	
Avli Tou Thodori	
Tamam	
M-eating	
Strofi	
Argo Taverna	
Naoussa Tavern	
Anogi	
Thanasis	
Katerina's Bar & Restaurant	
Salt & Pepper	
Metaxy Mas Tavern	

Best Websites to Research Further

Do some more research on the internet to plan your trip:

www.wikipedia.org/wiki/Greece
www.visitgreece.gr
www.greeka.com
www.greektravel.com
www.lonelyplanet.com/greece
www.roughguides.com/destinations/europe/greece
www.wikitravel.org/en/Greece
www.cycladia.com/travel-guides-greece/
www.nomadicmatt.com/travel-guides/Greece-travel-tips/

More places I want to visit on our trip

1. _____
2. _____
3. _____
4. _____
5. _____
6. _____
7. _____
8. _____
9. _____
10. _____
11. _____
12. _____
13. _____
14. _____
15. _____

Postcard List

Name:
Address:

Name:
Address:

Name:
Address:

Name:

Address:

Name:

Address:

Name:

Address:

Name:

Address:

Name:

Address:

Name:

Address:

Name:

Address:

Name:

Address:

Name:

Address:

Name:

Address:

Name:

Address:

Packing List

✓	This Journal
	Tickets
	Passport
	Money
	Chargers
	Batteries
	Book to read
	Camera
	Tablet
	Sun glasses
	Sun cream

	Toiletries
	Water
	Watch
	Snacks
	Umbrella
	Towel
	Guide book
	Kindle
	Jacket
	Medication
	Add more below

Greece Facts

- The official name of Greece is the Hellenic Republic

- The capital and largest city in Greece is Athens (Athina in Greek). Other major cities include Thessaloniki, Patras and Heraklion

- Greek has been spoken for more than 3,000 years, making it one of the oldest languages in Europe

- The Greek flag is popularly referred to as blue white. It includes nine blue-and-white horizontal stripes, which some scholars say stand for the nine syllables of the Greek motto "Eleftheria i Thanatos" or "Freedom or Death." In the upper left-hand corner of Greece's flag is the traditional Greek Orthodox cross

- Greece's currency, the drachma, was 2,650 years old and Europe's oldest currency. The drachma was replaced with the Euro in 2002

- Greece has the longest coastline on the Mediterranean Basin and the 11th longest coastline in the world at 13,676 km (8,498 miles) long

- The Pindus mountain range on the mainland contains one of the world's deepest gorges, Vikos Gorge, which plunges 3,600 feet (1,100 meters)

- Mount Olympus is Greece's highest mountain at 9,570 feet (2,917 meters). Ancient Greeks believed it was the home of the gods. Mount Olympus became the first national park in Greece

- Greece has more than 2,000 islands, of which approximately 170 are populated. Greece's largest island is Crete

- The first Olympic Games were held in the southern city of Olympia in 776 B.C. to honor Zeus, the king of the gods

- Football (soccer) is the national sport of Greece

- Olive trees have been cultivated in Greece for over 6,000 years. Every village has its own olive groves.

- Feta, which is made from goat's milk, is the Greece's national cheese. It dates back to the Homeric ages, and the average per-capita consumption of feta cheese in Greece is the highest in the world

- Haliacmon River (Aliakmon) is the longest river in Greece

Clothes & Shoe Sizes

Children's Shoe Sizes

UK	EUROPE	US	Japan
4	20	4½ or 5	12 ½
4 ½	21	5 or 5½	13
5	21 or 22	5½ or 6	13 ½
5 ½	22	6	13½ or 14
6	23	6½ or 7	14 or 14½
6 ½	23 or 24	7 ½	14½ or 15
7	24	7½ or 8	15
7 ½	25	8 or 9	15 ½
8	25 or 26	8½ or 9	16
8 ½	26	9½	16 ½
9	27	9½ or 10	16 ½ or 17
10	28	10½ or 11	17 ½
10½ or 11	29	11½ or 12	18
11 ½	30	12½	18 or 18 ½
12	31	13	19 or 19 ½
12 ½	31	13 or 13½	19 ½ or 20
13	32	1	20
13 ½	32 ½	1 ½	20 ½
1	33	1½ or 2	21
2	34	2½ or 3	22

Children's Clothing Sizes

UK	EUROPE	US	Australia
12m	80cm	12-18m	12m
18m	80-86cm	18-24m	18m
24m	86-92cm	23-24m	2
2-3	92-98cm	2T	3
3-4	98-104cm	4T	4
3-5	104-110cm	5	5
5-6	110-116cm	6	6
6-7	116-122cm	6X-7	7
7-8	122-128cm	7 to 8	8
8-9	128-134cm	9 to 10	9
9-10	134-140cm	10	10
10-11	140-146cm	11	11
11-12	146-152cm	14	12

Women's Shoe Sizes

UK	EUROPE	US	Japan
3	35 ½	5	22 ½
3 ½	36	5 ½	23
4	37	6	23
4 ½	37 ½	6 ½	23 ½
5	38	7	24
5 ½	39	7 ½	24
6	39 ½	8	24 ½
6 ½	40	8 ½	25
7	41	9 ½	25 ½
7 ½	41 ½	10	26
8	42	10 ½	26 ½

Women's Clothes Sizes

UK	US	Japan	France / Spain	Germany	Greece	Australia
6/8	6	7-9	36	34	40	8
10	8	9-11	38	36	42	10
12	10	11-13	40	38	44	12
14	12	13-15	42	39	46	14
16	14	15-17	44	40	48	16
18	16	17-19	46	42	50	18
20	18	19-21	48	44	52	20

Men's Shoe Sizes

UK	EUROPE	US	Japan
6	38 ½	6 ½	24 ½
6 ½	39	7	25
7	40	7 ½	25 ½
7 ½	41	8	26
8	42	8 ½	27 ½
8 ½	43	9	27 ½
9	43 ½	9 ½	28
9 ½	44	10	28 ½
10	44	10 ½	28 ½
10 ½	44 ½	11	29
11	45	12	29 ½

Men's Suit / Coat / Sweater Sizes

UK / US / Aus	EU / Japan	General
32	42	Small
34	44	Small
36	46	Small
38	48	Medium
40	50	Large
42	52	Large
44	54	Extra Large
46	56	Extra Large

Men's Pants / Trouser Sizes (Waist)

UK / US	Europe
32	81 cm
34	86 cm
36	91 cm
38	97 cm
40	102 cm
42	107 cm

We have included another copy of this at the back of the book, so you can find it quickly again when you are in Greece

Greece Trip Diary
Write a daily diary during your trip

Day 1

Date: _____   **Weather:** _____

Day 2

Date: _____   **Weather:** _____

Day 3

Date: _____ **Weather:** _____

Day 4

Date: _____   **Weather:** _____

Day 5

Tip! Send your postcards

Date: _____   **Weather:** _____

Day 6

Date: _____   **Weather:** _____

Day 7

Date: _____   **Weather:** _____

Day 8

Date: _____   **Weather:** _____

Day 9

Date: _____   **Weather:** _____

Day 10

Date: _____ **Weather:** _____

Day 11

Date: _____   **Weather:** _____

Day 12

Date: _____   **Weather:** _____

Day 13

Date: _____   Weather: _____

Day 14

Date: _____   **Weather:** _____

Day 15

Date: _____   **Weather:** _____

Day 16

Date: _____   Weather: _____

Day 17

Date: _____   Weather: _____

Day 18

Date: _____ **Weather:** _____

Day 19

Date: _____ **Weather:** _____

Day 20

Date: _____   **Weather:** _____

Day 21

Date: _____   Weather: _____

Memories of your Trip

Things I will remember from the trip

Favorite Places visited on the Trip

People I Met

Name:
Address:
Tel:
email:

Name:
Address:
Tel:
email:

Name:
Address:
Tel:
email:

Name:
Address:
Tel:
email:

Name:
Address:
Tel:
email:

Name:
Address:
Tel:
email:

Name:
Address:
Tel:
email:

Name:
Address:
Tel:
email:

Name:
Address:
Tel:
email:

Name:
Address:
Tel:
email:

Name:
Address:
Tel:
email:

126

We hope you enjoyed your trip to Greece

Please leave us a review if you found this Journal useful

Check out our useful resources on the next few pages

Clothes & Shoe Sizes

Children's Shoe Sizes

UK	EUROPE	US	Japan
4	20	4½ or 5	12 ½
4 ½	21	5 or 5½	13
5	21 or 22	5½ or 6	13 ½
5 ½	22	6	13½ or 14
6	23	6½ or 7	14 or 14½
6 ½	23 or 24	7 ½	14½ or 15
7	24	7½ or 8	15
7 ½	25	8 or 9	15 ½
8	25 or 26	8½ or 9	16
8 ½	26	9½	16 ½
9	27	9½ or 10	16 ½ or 17
10	28	10½ or 11	17 ½
10½ or 11	29	11½ or 12	18
11 ½	30	12½	18 or 18 ½
12	31	13	19 or 19 ½
12 ½	31	13 or 13½	19 ½ or 20
13	32	1	20
13 ½	32 ½	1 ½	20 ½
1	33	1½ or 2	21
2	34	2½ or 3	22

Children's Clothing Sizes

UK	EUROPE	US	Australia
12m	80cm	12-18m	12m
18m	80-86cm	18-24m	18m
24m	86-92cm	23-24m	2
2-3	92-98cm	2T	3
3-4	98-104cm	4T	4
3-5	104-110cm	5	5
5-6	110-116cm	6	6
6-7	116-122cm	6X-7	7
7-8	122-128cm	7 to 8	8
8-9	128-134cm	9 to 10	9
9-10	134-140cm	10	10
10-11	140-146cm	11	11
11-12	146-152cm	14	12

Women's Shoe Sizes

UK	EUROPE	US	Japan
3	35 ½	5	22 ½
3 ½	36	5 ½	23
4	37	6	23
4 ½	37 ½	6 ½	23 ½
5	38	7	24
5 ½	39	7 ½	24
6	39 ½	8	24 ½
6 ½	40	8 ½	25
7	41	9 ½	25 ½
7 ½	41 ½	10	26
8	42	10 ½	26 ½

Women's Clothes Sizes

UK	US	Japan	France / Spain	Germany	Greece	Australia
6/8	6	7-9	36	34	40	8
10	8	9-11	38	36	42	10
12	10	11-13	40	38	44	12
14	12	13-15	42	39	46	14
16	14	15-17	44	40	48	16
18	16	17-19	46	42	50	18
20	18	19-21	48	44	52	20

Men's Shoe Sizes

UK	EUROPE	US	Japan
6	38 ½	6 ½	24 ½
6 ½	39	7	25
7	40	7 ½	25 ½
7 ½	41	8	26
8	42	8 ½	27 ½
8 ½	43	9	27 ½
9	43 ½	9 ½	28
9 ½	44	10	28 ½
10	44	10 ½	28 ½
10 ½	44 ½	11	29
11	45	12	29 ½

Men's Suit / Coat / Sweater Sizes

UK / US / Aus	EU / Japan	General
32	42	Small
34	44	Small
36	46	Small
38	48	Medium
40	50	Large
42	52	Large
44	54	Extra Large
46	56	Extra Large

Men's Pants / Trouser Sizes (Waist)

UK / US	Europe
32	81 cm
34	86 cm
36	91 cm
38	97 cm
40	102 cm
42	107 cm

Common Translations

English	French	Spanish	Italian
Hello	Bonjour	Hola	Ciao
Goodbye	Au revoir	Adiós	Arrivederci
Yes	Oui	Sí	Si
No	Non	No	No
Please	S'il-vous-plaît	Por favor	Per favore
Thank you	Merci	Gracias	Grazie
Excuse me	Excusez-moi	Perdón	Mi scusi
How much	Combien	Cuánto	Quanto
My name is	Mon nom est	Mi nombre es	Io mi chiamo
Where is	Où est	Dónde está	Dov'è
The bank	La banque	El banco	La banca
The toilet	Les toilettes	El baño	Il bagno

German	Japanese	Mandarin	Hindi
Hallo	Kon'nichiwa	Ni hao	Namaste
Auf Wiedersehen	Sayonara	Zaijian	Alavida
Ja	Hai	Shi de	Ham
Nein	Ie	Meiyou	Nahim
Bitte	Onegaishimasu	Qing	Krpaya
Vielen Dank	Arigato	Xiexie	Dhan'yavada
Entschuldigung	Sumimasen	Duoshao	Mujhe mapha karem
Wie viel	Ikura	Wo de mingzi shi	Kitana
Mein Name ist	Watashinonamaeha	Nali	Mera nama hai
Wo ist	Doko ni aru	Yinhang	Kaham hai
Die Bank	Ginko	Yinhang	Bainka
Die Toilette	Toire	Cesuo	Saucalaya

Notes:

CPSIA information can be obtained
at www.ICGtesting.com
Printed in the USA
FSOW03n2038081216
28358FS